GYMNASTICS COLORING BOOK

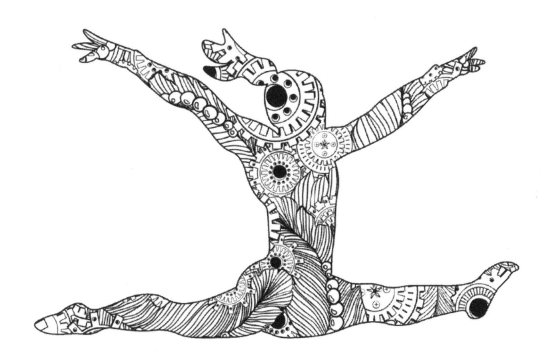

Compilation by Cora Delmonico

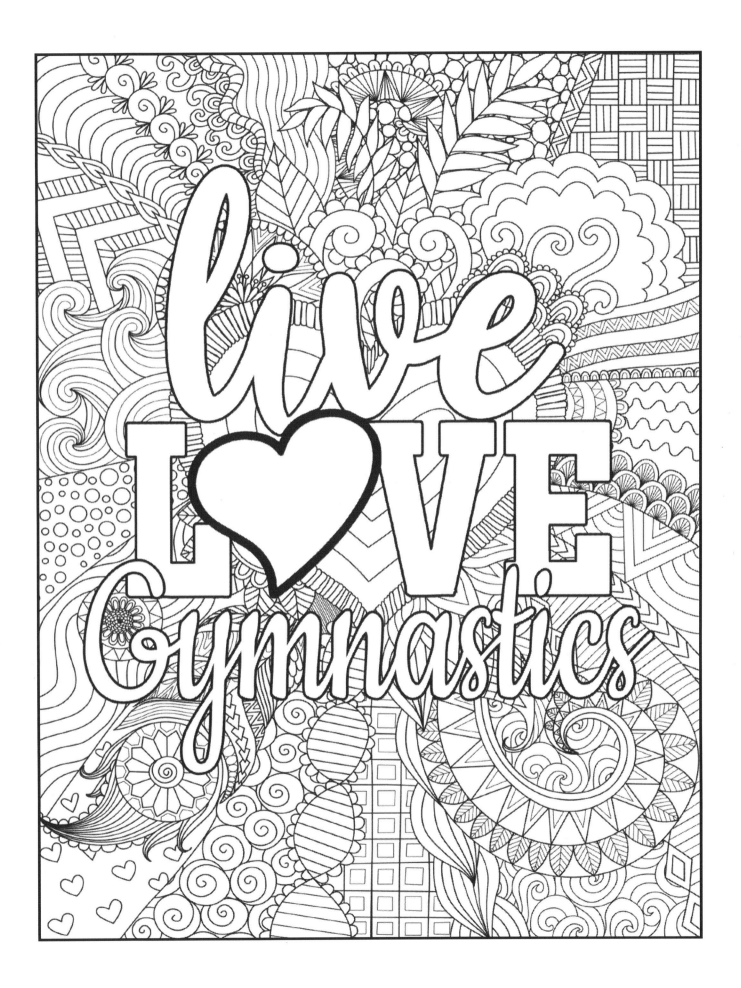

Beam

perfect
10!

Stick the Landing

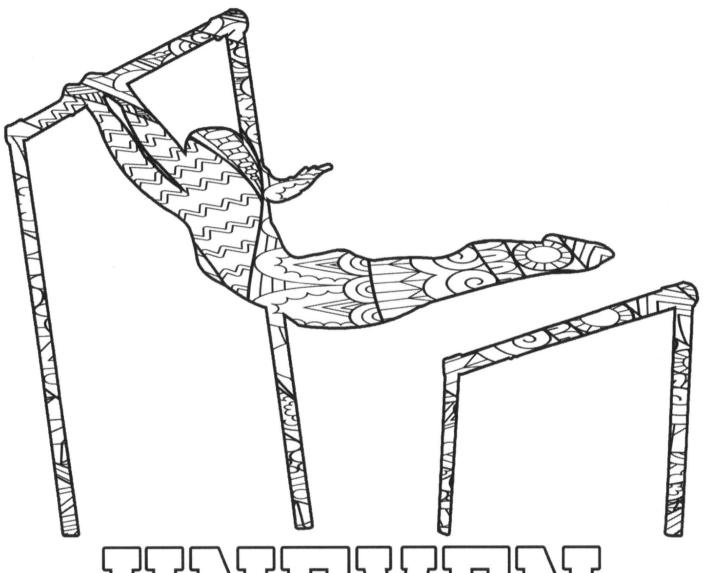

UNEVEN
BARS

GYMNASTICS
GYMNASTICS
GYMNASTICS
GYMNASTICS
GYMNASTICS
GYMNASTICS
GYMNASTICS

Warning:

I might flip out!

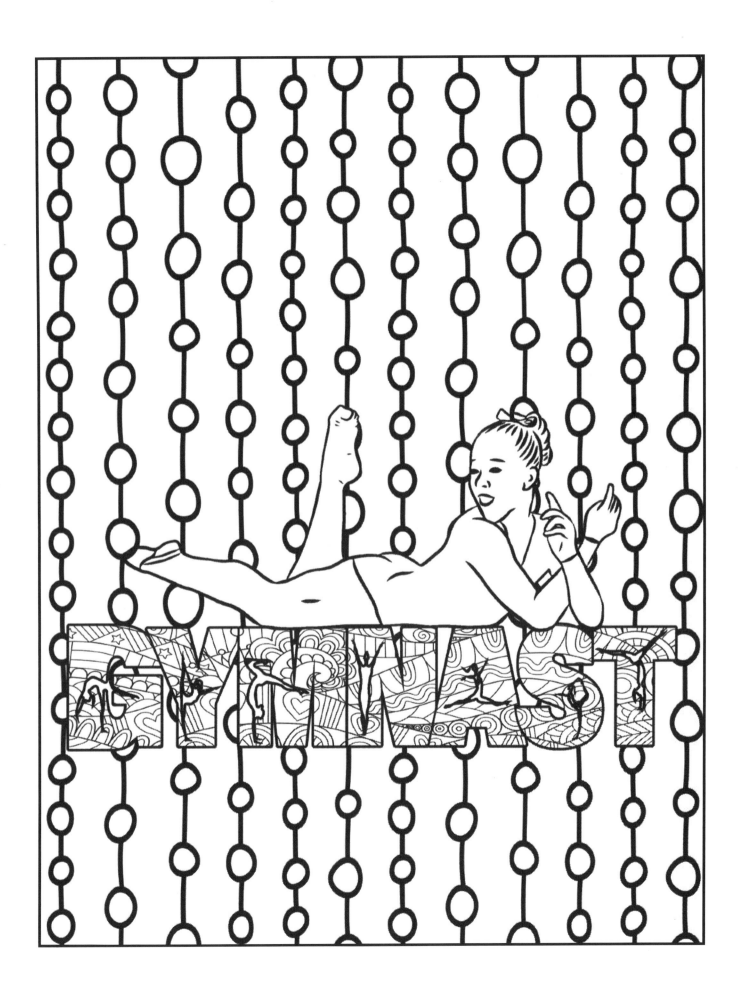

I Tumble
For You!

VauLt ♡

FloOr

UneVen Bars

BEam

Floor

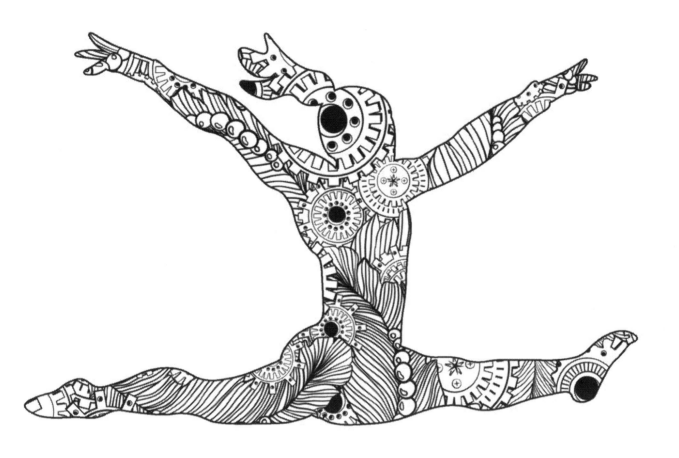

Tear this page out and place between your coloring pages to prevent the ink from bleeding through if you choose to use markers.
Use again and again!

Tear this page out and place between your coloring pages to prevent the ink from bleeding through if you choose to use markers.
Use again and again!

Tear this page out and place between your coloring pages to prevent the ink from bleeding through if you choose to use markers.
Use again and again!

Made in the USA
Las Vegas, NV
04 November 2024

11122896R00044